Squirrel Practice

This Logbook Belongs To

_____

*"In theory there is no difference between theory and practice,
but in practice there is."*

Yogi Berra, American baseball player 1925-2015

Congratulations

Welcome to Squirrel Practice!

No time to practice? No problem! Have fun with these speedy Brain Hacks.
I relay on them constantly, especially when "Oh Shiny!" so many performances are happening!
Having a Clear Goal, Knowing What to Do, How Many Times to Do It, and WHEN
makes practice super easy with fast results. Log it here and you can see for yourself!
We *should* all know that LISTENING is Essential!
And that the timing of Sleep is also a critical part of the puzzle.
How about Getting it Right The First Time? How can you even do "First Time Practice" anyway?
This is definitely a Squirrel Hack. They fly from pillar to post with no room for error -
at least in my garden, as they steal oranges and toss them into the pool, with us in it!
Leverage that Quick Reaction Squirrel Skill using "Interleaved Practice."
Mix up the order of your practice nuggets, then follow a different path each day.
Bonus Challenge: Test yourselves by filming "1st Pass Videos" to start a practice session.

Leslie Brown Katz, violinist
Los Angeles Opera, Suzuki Teacher, and
Proud Mama of three Precocious Squirrels

How To Use Things in This Logbook

At the Lesson - Fill in your Clear Practice Tasks, Practice Nuggets, and what your Teacher wants you to Focus On.

During the Week:
Log your Practice Dates in a Leaf corresponding to the Time of Day

AM

PM

Clear Practice Tasks

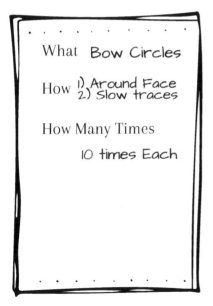

What Bow Circles

How 1) Around Face
      2) Slow traces

How Many Times

        10 times Each

Staff to write Practice Nuggets

"Aha!" Alert
for the Week

Thumbs!

"1st Time" Interleaved Practice
Choose 5 things to do
5x's The First Time!
Follow the Acorn Trail starting
in any direction each day.

Questions for next Lesson?

What

How

How Many Times

What

How

How Many Times

What

How

How Many Times

♪♫ Listen Like a Maniac!

Questions for next Lesson?

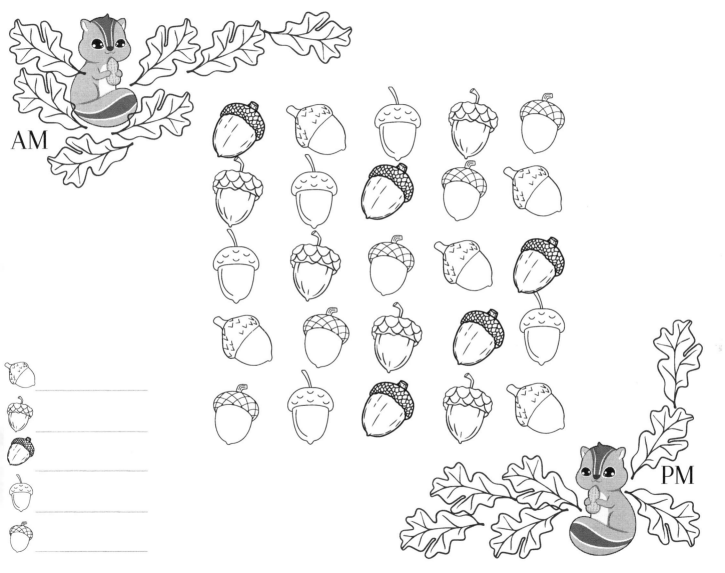

AM

PM

Date

What

How

How Many Times

What

How

How Many Times

What

How

How Many Times

Listen Like a Maniac!

Questions for next Lesson?

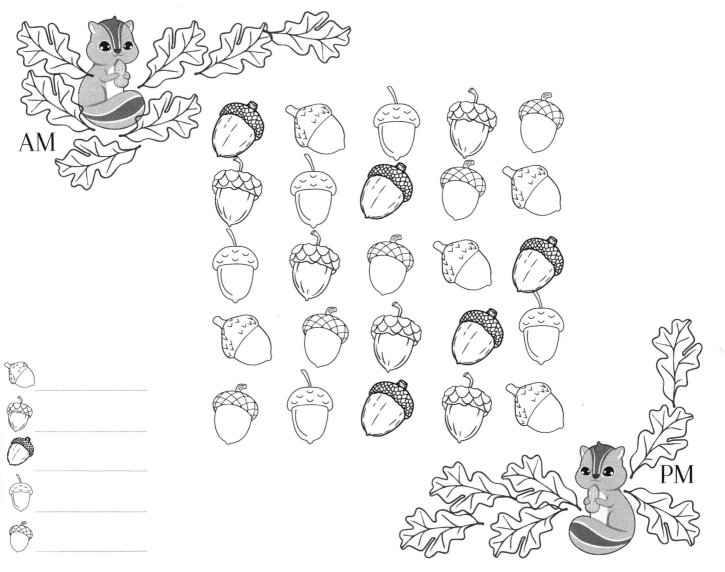

Date

What

How

How Many Times

What

How

How Many Times

What

How

How Many Times

♪ Listen Like a Maniac!

Questions for next Lesson?

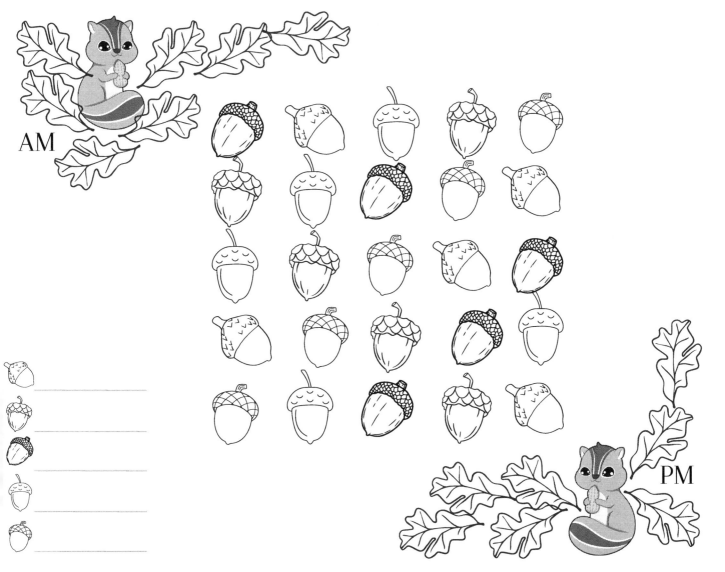

Date

What

How

How Many Times

What

How

How Many Times

What

How

How Many Times

♪ Listen Like a Maniac!

Questions for next Lesson?

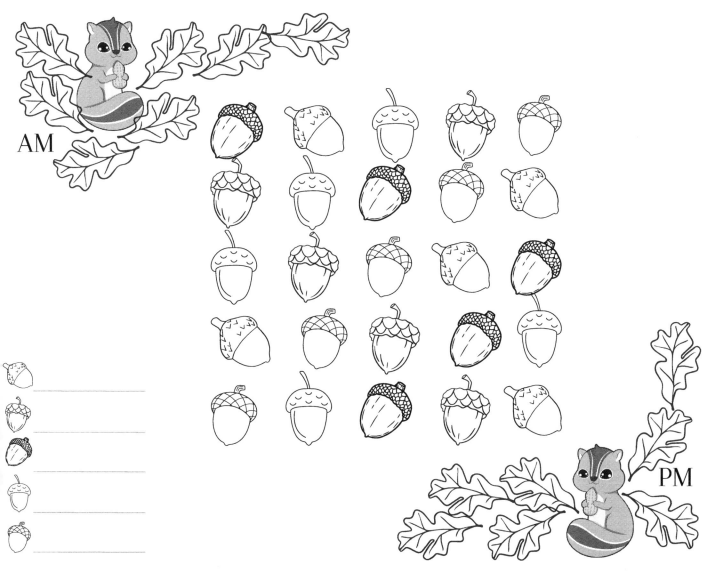

Date

What

How

How Many Times

What

How

How Many Times

What

How

How Many Times

Listen Like a Maniac!

Questions for next Lesson?

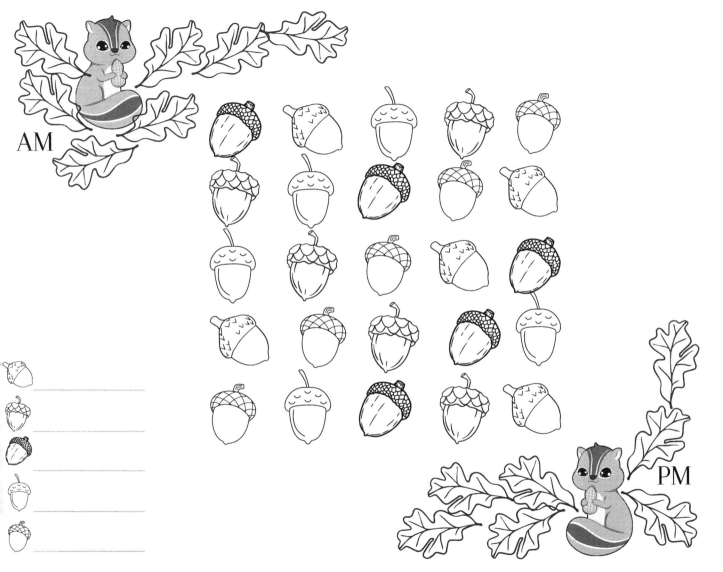

Date _____

What

How

How Many Times

What

How

How Many Times

What

How

How Many Times

♪♫ Listen Like a Maniac!

Questions for next Lesson?

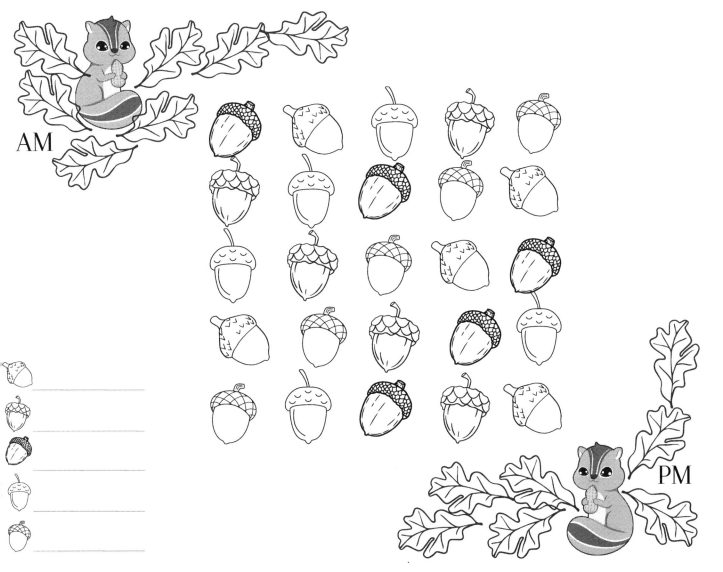

Date

What

How

How Many Times

What

How

How Many Times

What

How

How Many Times

Questions for next Lesson?

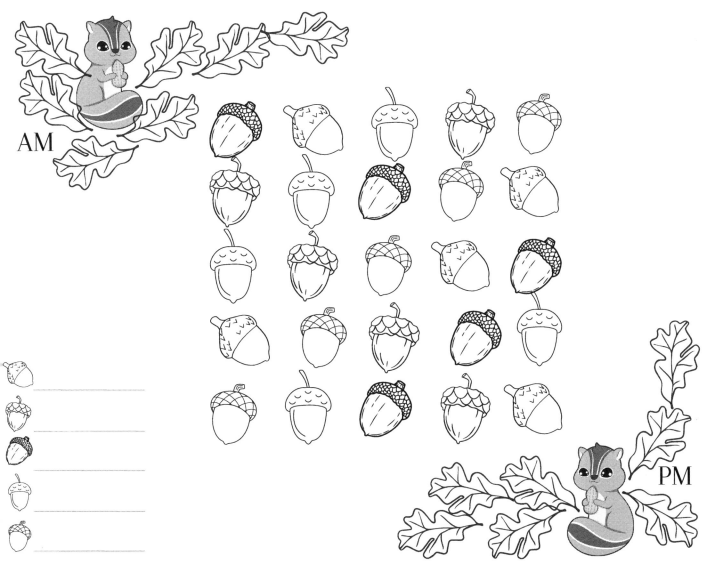

Date

What

How

How Many Times

What

How

How Many Times

What

How

How Many Times

♪♫ Listen Like a Maniac!

Questions for next Lesson?

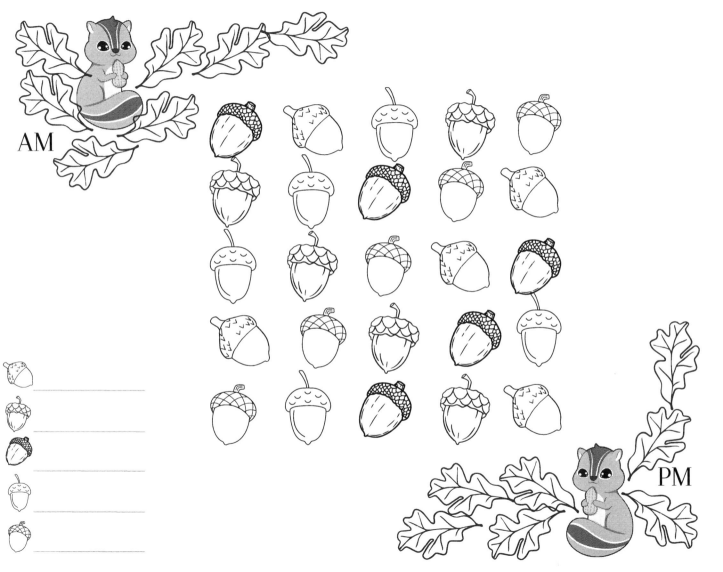

AM

PM

Date

What

How

How Many Times

What

How

How Many Times

What

How

How Many Times

Listen Like a Maniac!

Questions for next Lesson?

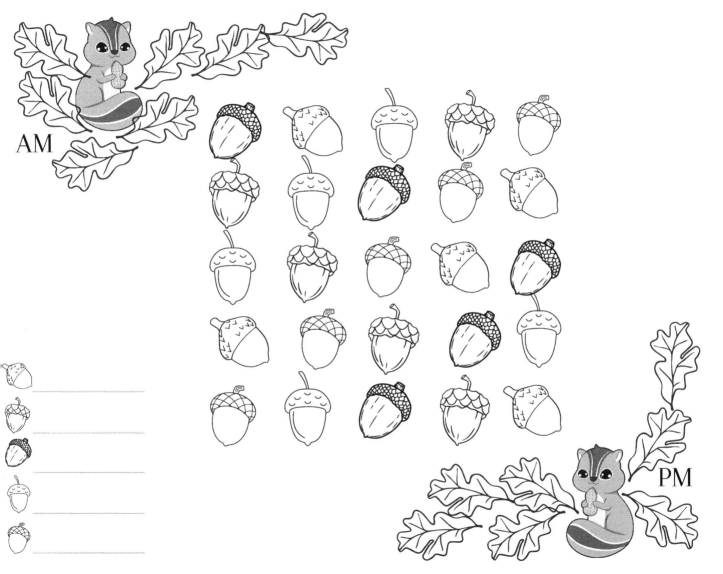

AM

PM

Date

What

How

How Many Times

What

How

How Many Times

What

How

How Many Times

Listen Like a Maniac!

Questions for next Lesson?

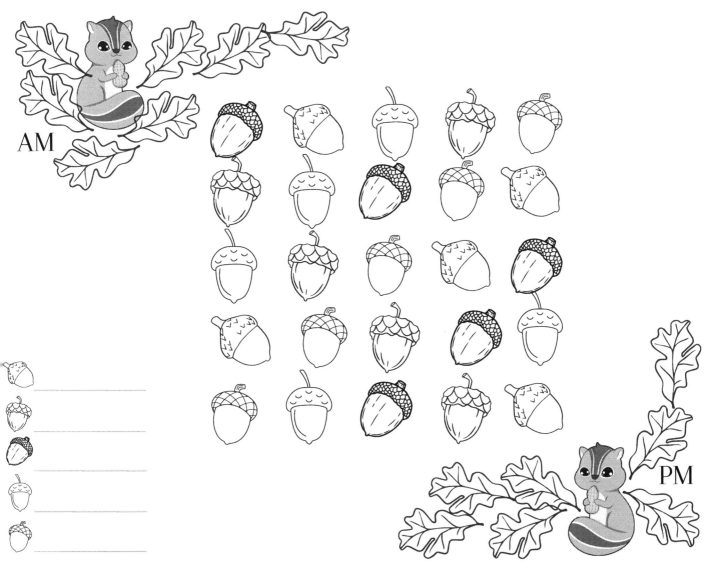

What

How

How Many Times

What

How

How Many Times

What

How

How Many Times

♪♫ Listen Like a Maniac!

Questions for next Lesson?

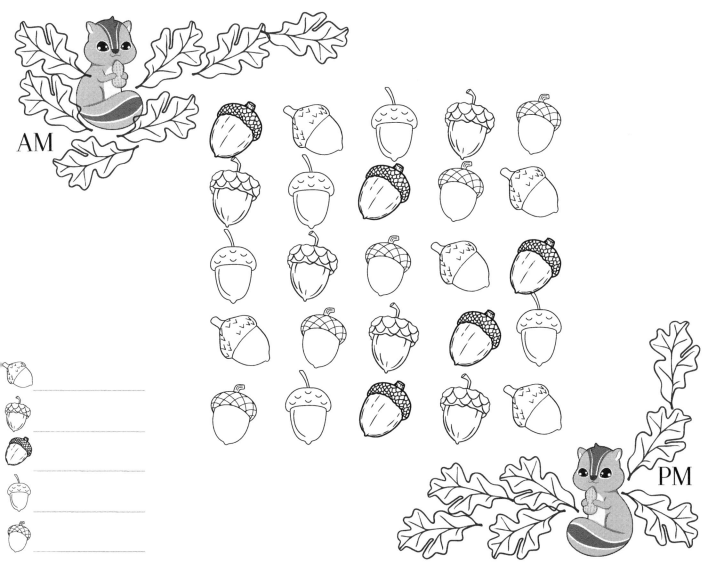

AM

PM

What

How

How Many Times

What

How

How Many Times

What

How

How Many Times

♪♫♪ Listen Like a Maniac!

Questions for next Lesson?

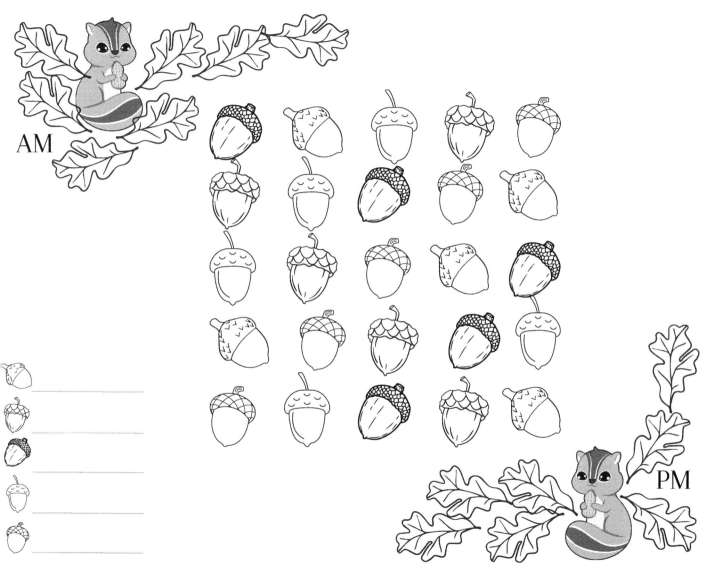

Date

What

How

How Many Times

What

How

How Many Times

What

How

How Many Times

Questions for next Lesson?

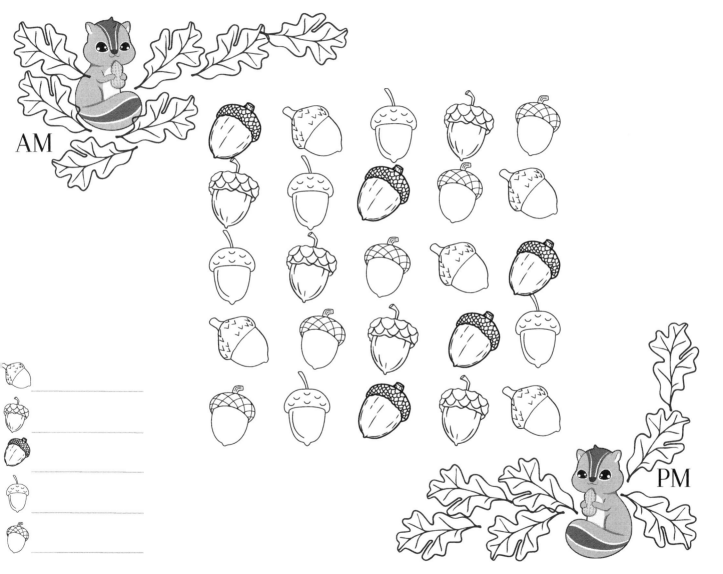

Date

What

How

How Many Times

What

How

How Many Times

What

How

How Many Times

Listen Like a Maniac!

Questions for next Lesson?

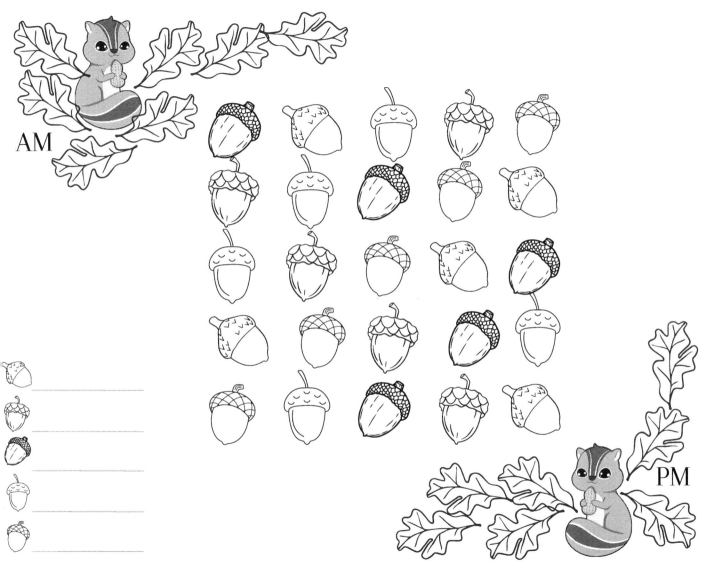

Date _____

What

How

How Many Times

What

How

How Many Times

What

How

How Many Times

Questions for next Lesson?

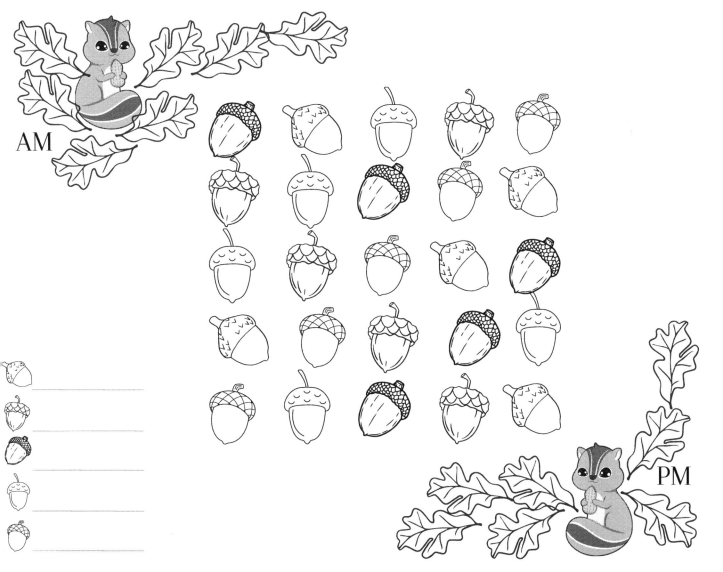

AM

PM

Date

What

How

How Many Times

What

How

How Many Times

What

How

How Many Times

Listen Like a Maniac!

Questions for next Lesson?

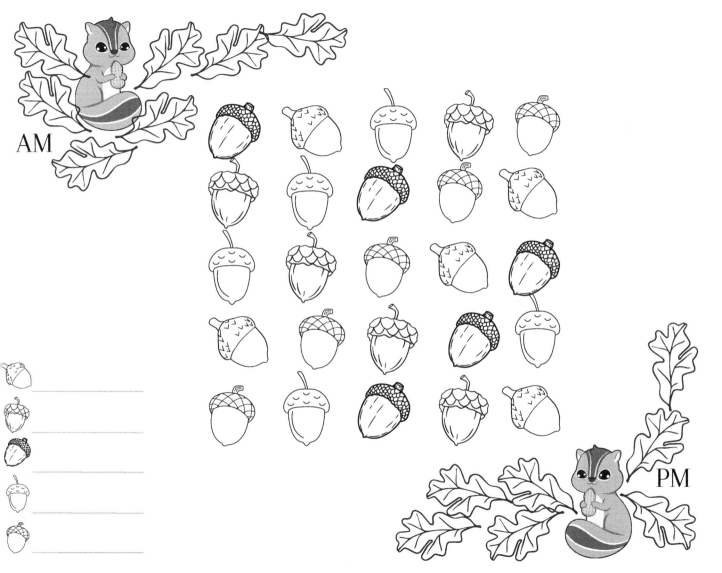

Date

What

How

How Many Times

What

How

How Many Times

What

How

How Many Times

♪♫ Listen Like a Maniac!

Questions for next Lesson?

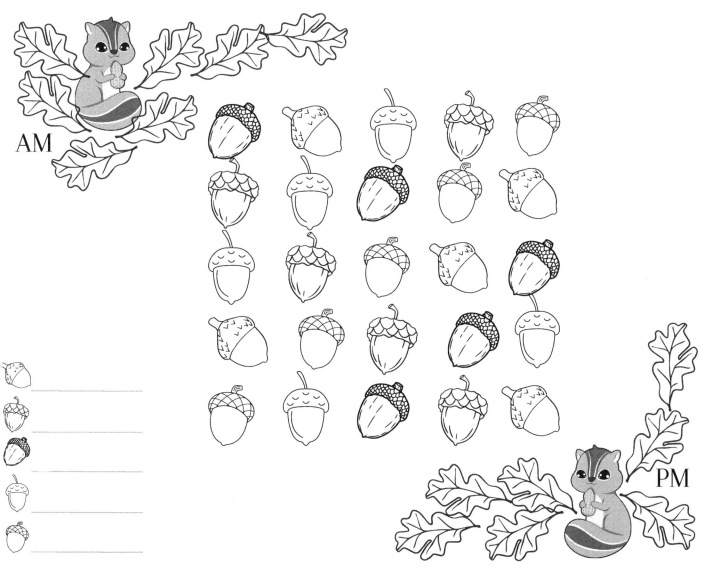

AM

PM

Date

What

How

How Many Times

What

How

How Many Times

What

How

How Many Times

Questions for next Lesson?

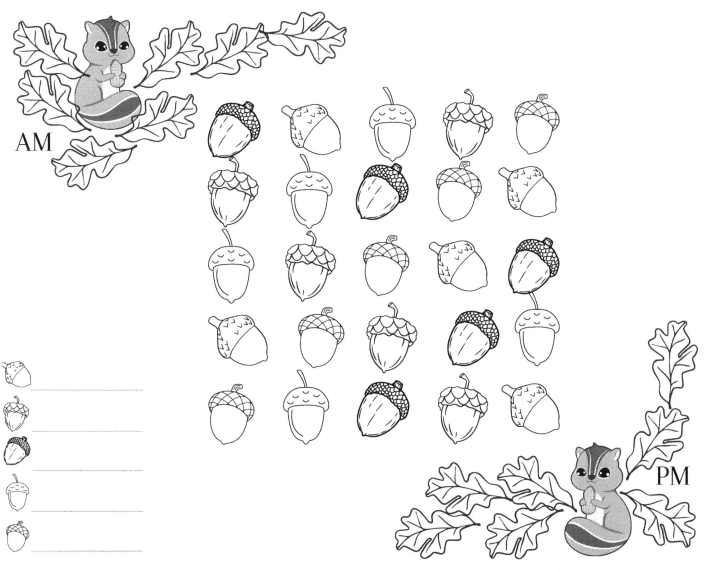

AM

PM

Date

What

How

How Many Times

What

How

How Many Times

What

How

How Many Times

♪♫ Listen Like a Maniac!

Questions for next Lesson?

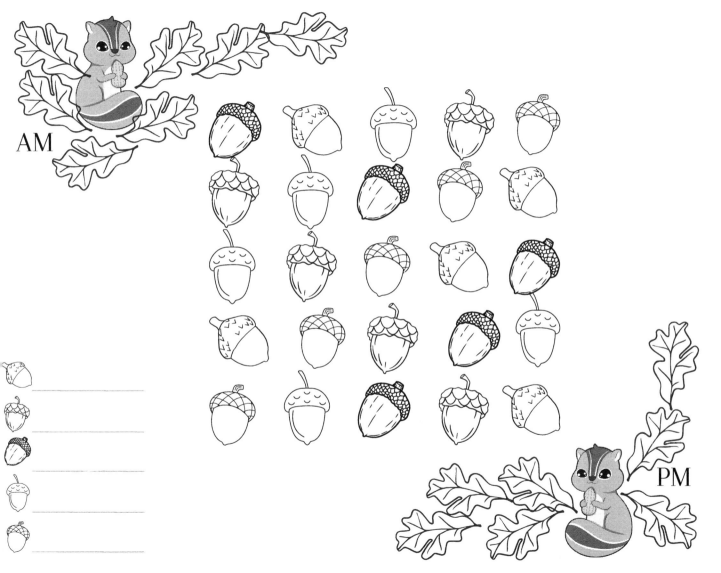

Date

What

How

How Many Times

What

How

How Many Times

What

How

How Many Times

Listen Like a Maniac!

Questions for next Lesson?

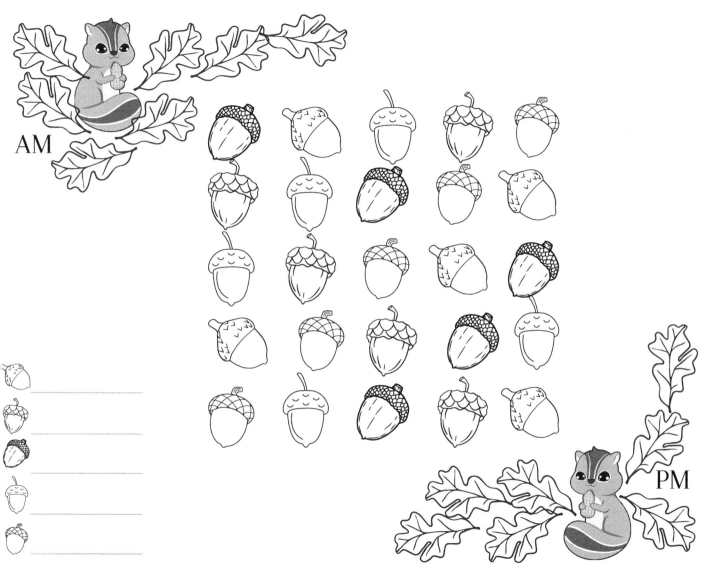

Date

What

How

How Many Times

What

How

How Many Times

What

How

How Many Times

♪♫ Listen Like a Maniac!

Questions for next Lesson?

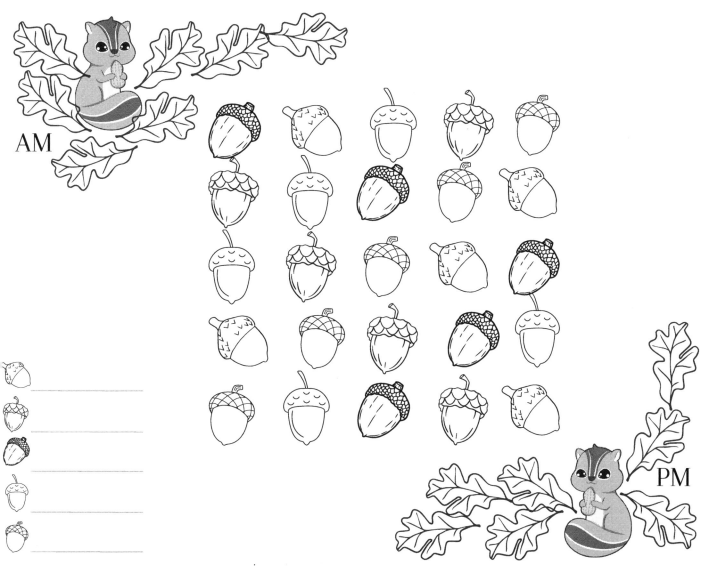

Date

What

How

How Many Times

What

How

How Many Times

What

How

How Many Times

Listen Like a Maniac!

Questions for next Lesson?

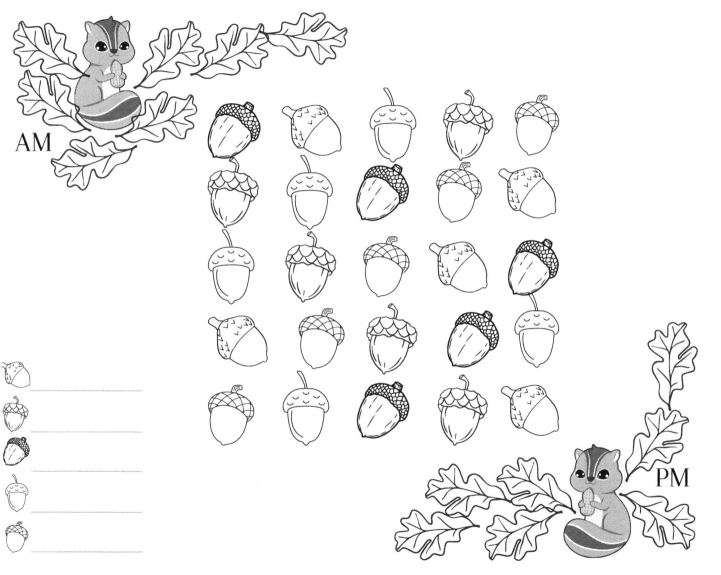

Date

What

How

How Many Times

What

How

How Many Times

What

How

How Many Times

♪♫ Listen Like a Maniac!

Questions for next Lesson?

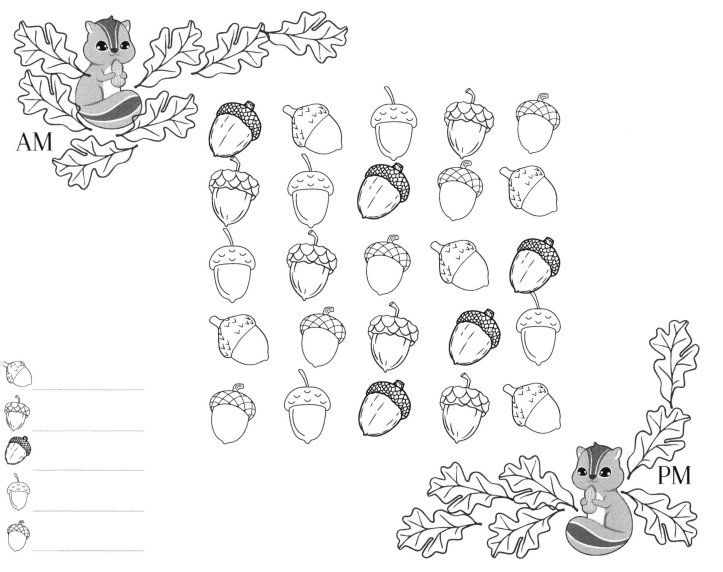

Date _____

What

How

How Many Times

What

How

How Many Times

What

How

How Many Times

♪♫ Listen Like a Maniac!

Questions for next Lesson?

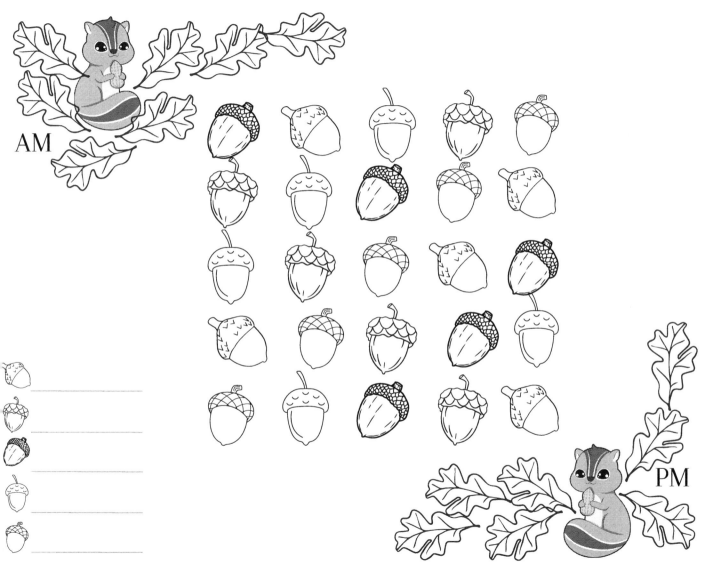

Date

What

How

How Many Times

What

How

How Many Times

What

How

How Many Times

Listen Like a Maniac!

Questions for next Lesson?

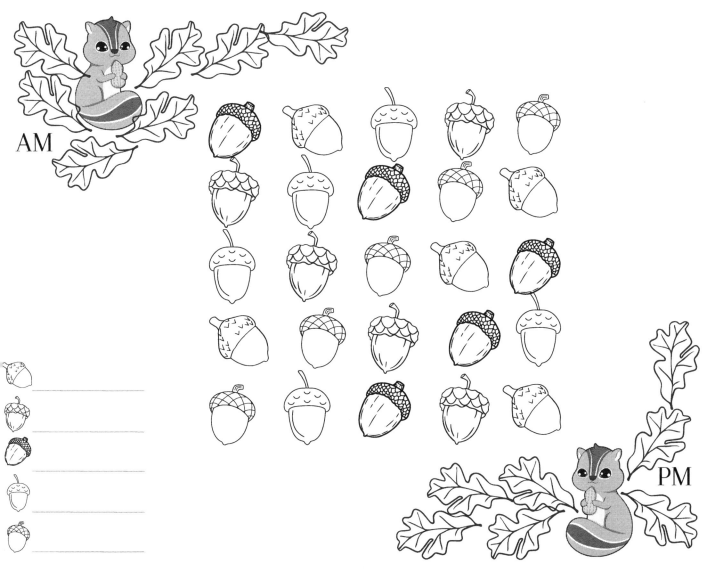

What

How

How Many Times

What

How

How Many Times

What

How

How Many Times

Listen Like a Maniac!

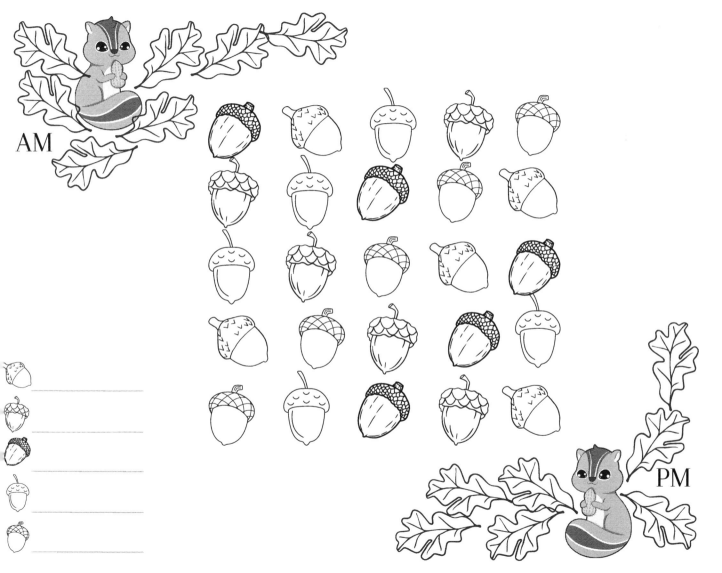

Date

What

How

How Many Times

What

How

How Many Times

What

How

How Many Times

Questions for next Lesson?

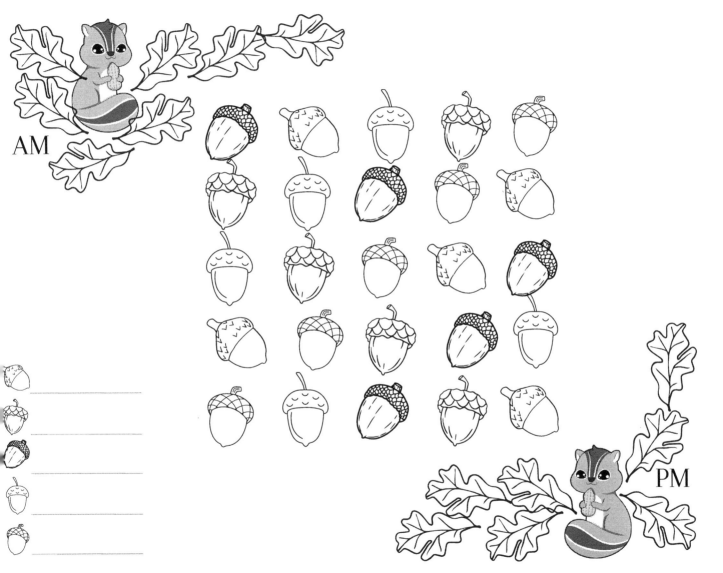

AM

PM

Date _____

What

How

How Many Times

What

How

How Many Times

What

How

How Many Times

♪♫ Listen Like a Maniac!

Questions for next Lesson?

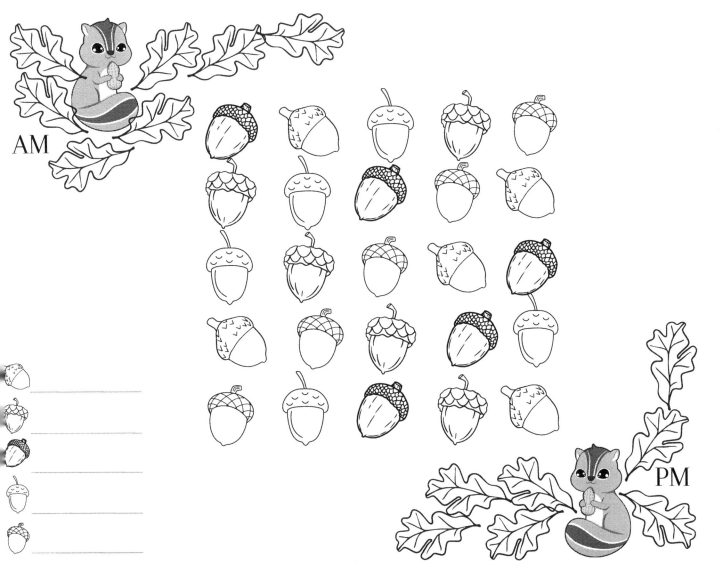

Date _____

What

How

How Many Times

What

How

How Many Times

What

How

How Many Times

♪♪ Listen Like a Maniac!

Questions for next Lesson?

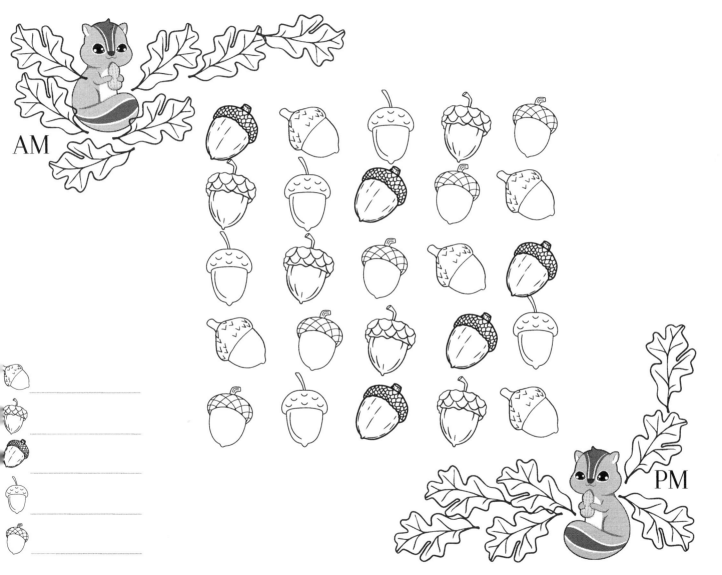

AM

PM

Date _____

What

How

How Many Times

What

How

How Many Times

What

How

How Many Times

Questions for next Lesson?

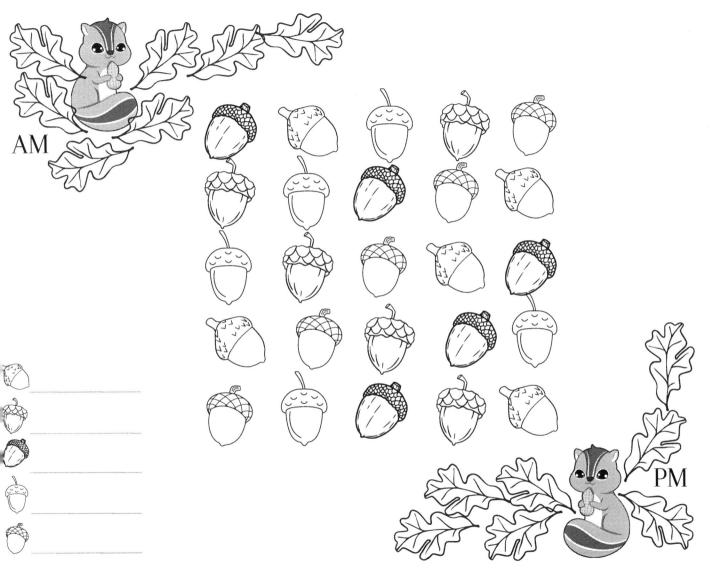

AM

PM

Date _____

What

How

How Many Times

What

How

How Many Times

What

How

How Many Times

♪♫ Listen Like a Maniac!

Questions for next Lesson?

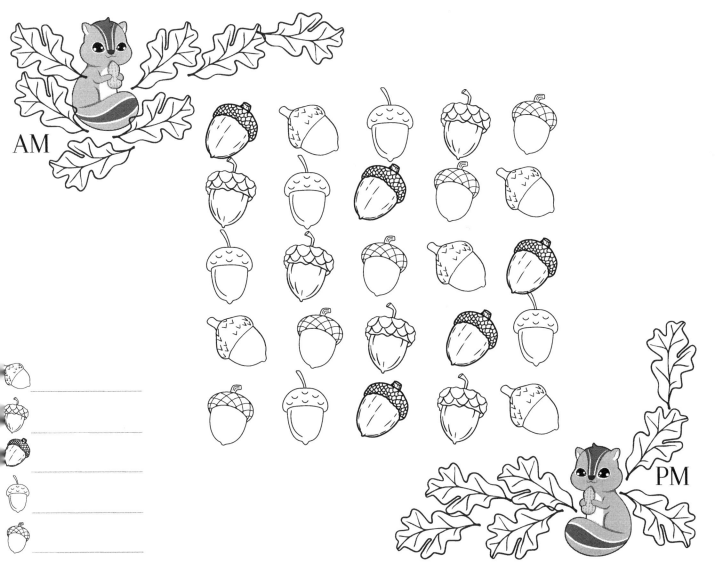

Date

What

How

How Many Times

What

How

How Many Times

What

How

How Many Times

♪♫ Listen Like a Maniac!

Questions for next Lesson?

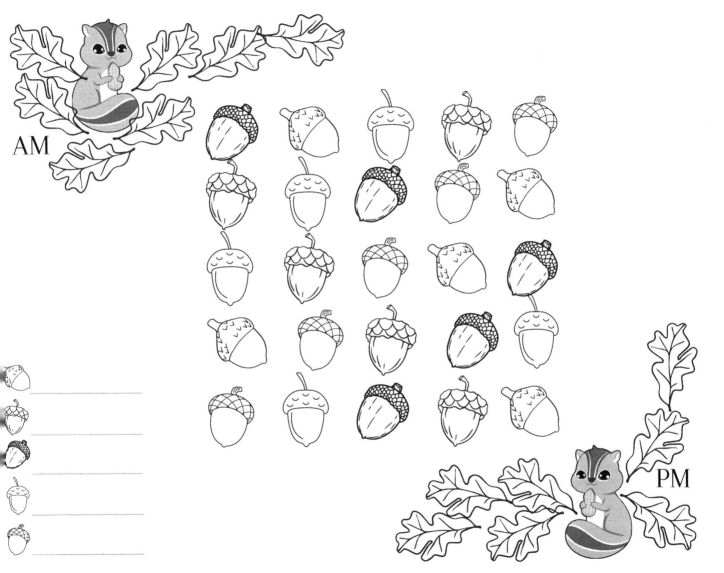

Date _____

What

How

How Many Times

What

How

How Many Times

What

How

How Many Times

Questions for next Lesson?

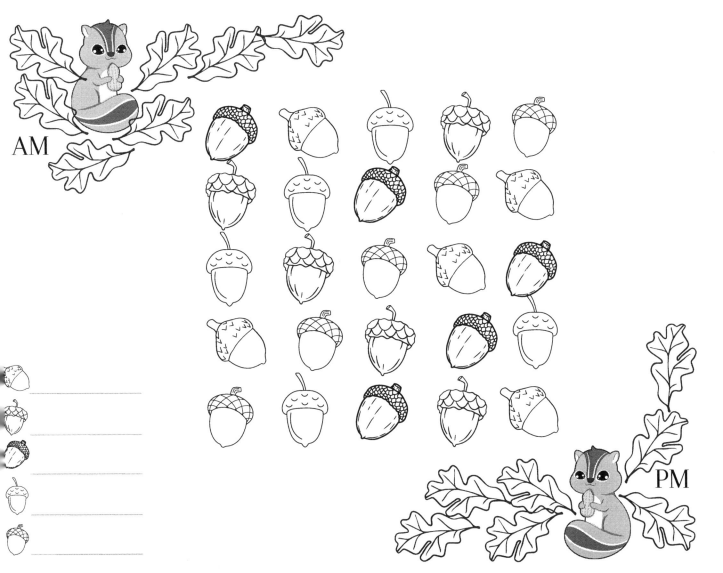

Date

What

How

How Many Times

What

How

How Many Times

What

How

How Many Times

Questions for next Lesson?

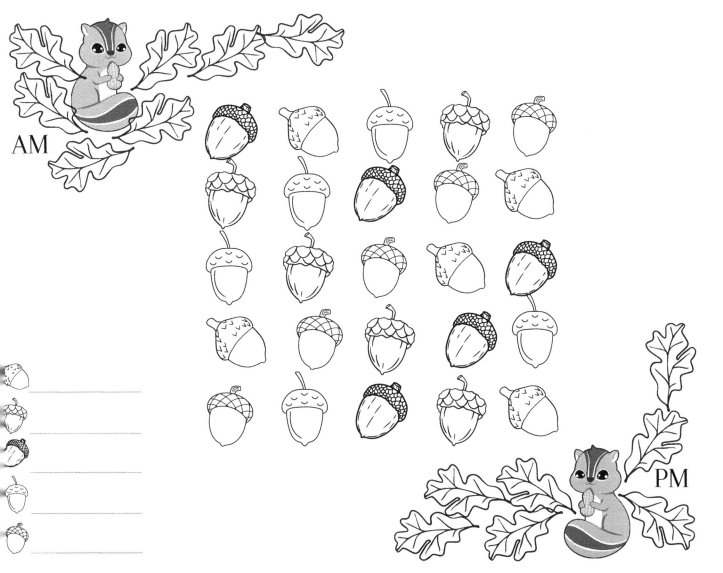

AM

PM

Date _____

What

How

How Many Times

What

How

How Many Times

What

How

How Many Times

🎵 Listen Like a Maniac!

Questions for next Lesson?

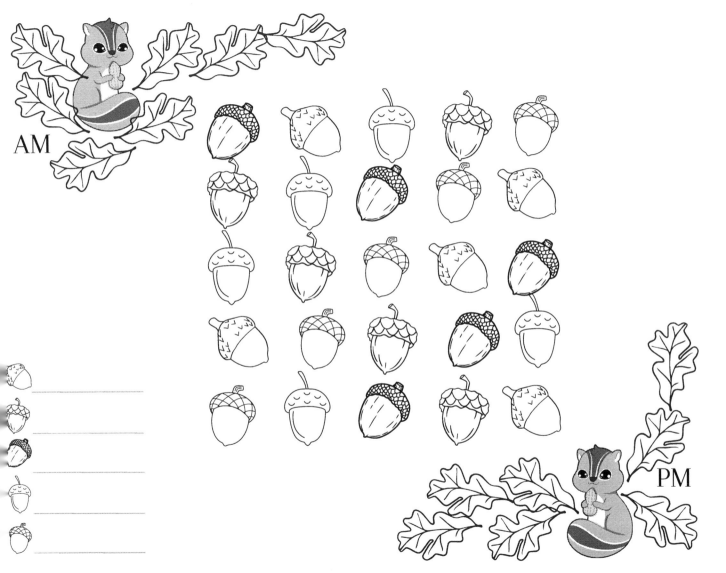

Date _____

What

How

How Many Times

What

How

How Many Times

What

How

How Many Times

Questions for next Lesson?

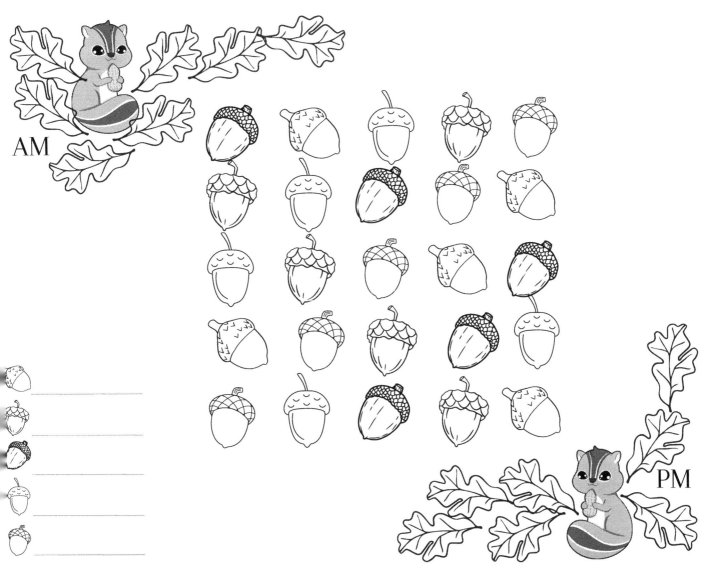

Date

What

How

How Many Times

What

How

How Many Times

What

How

How Many Times

Listen Like a Maniac!

Questions for next Lesson?

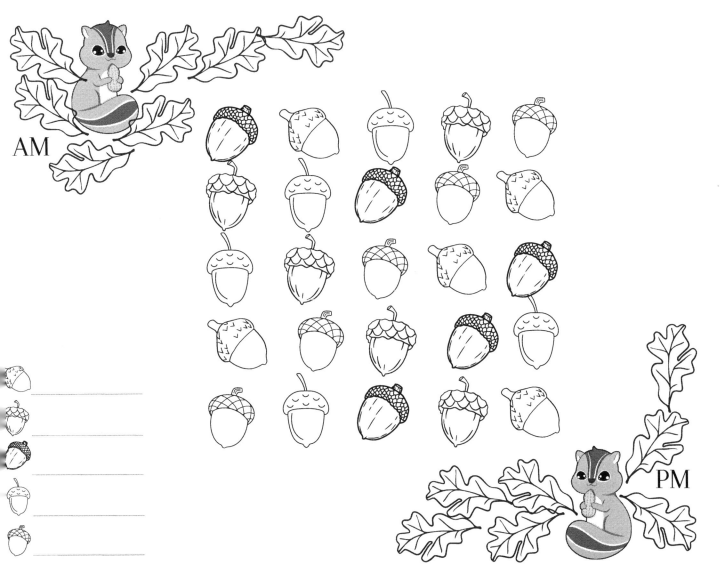

What

How

How Many Times

What

How

How Many Times

What

How

How Many Times

Listen Like a Maniac!

Questions for next Lesson?

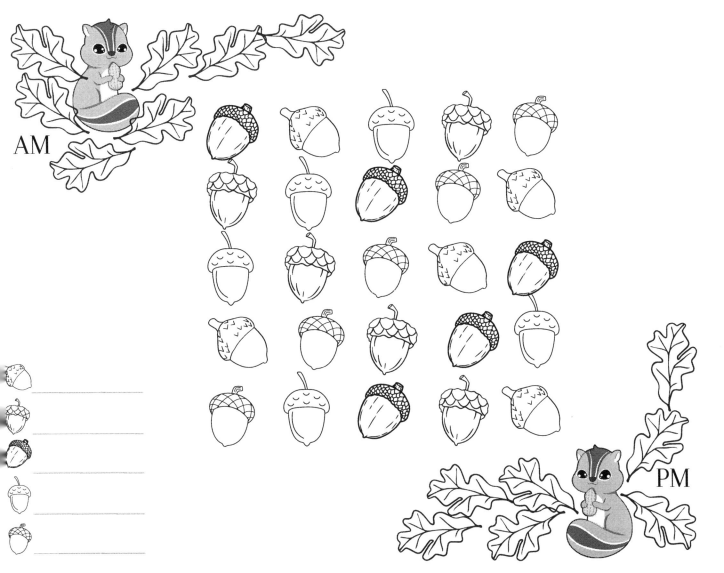

Date _____

What

How

How Many Times

What

How

How Many Times

What

How

How Many Times

Questions for next Lesson?

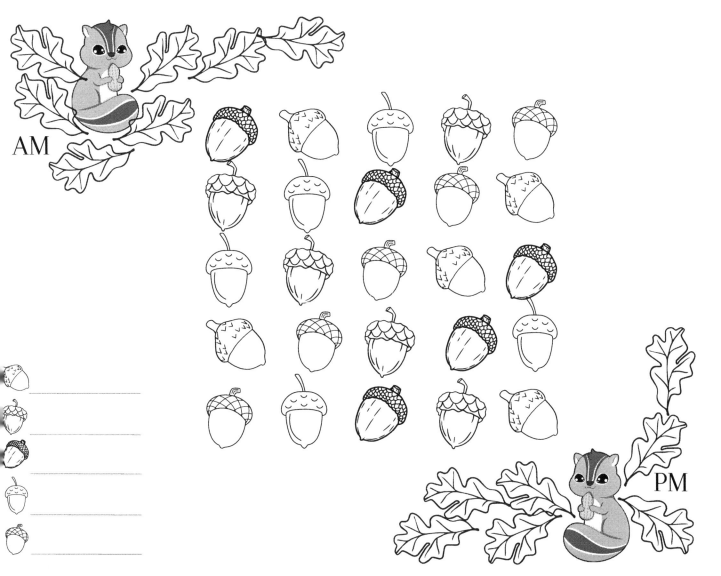

Date

What

How

How Many Times

What

How

How Many Times

What

How

How Many Times

♪♫ Listen Like a Maniac!

Questions for next Lesson?

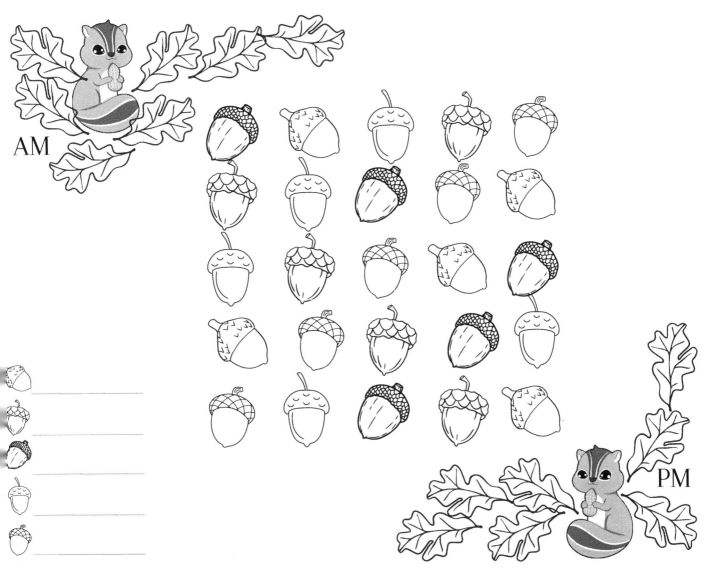

Date

What

How

How Many Times

What

How

How Many Times

What

How

How Many Times

♪♫ Listen Like a Maniac!

Questions for next Lesson?

Date

What

How

How Many Times

What

How

How Many Times

What

How

How Many Times

Listen Like a Maniac!

Questions for next Lesson?

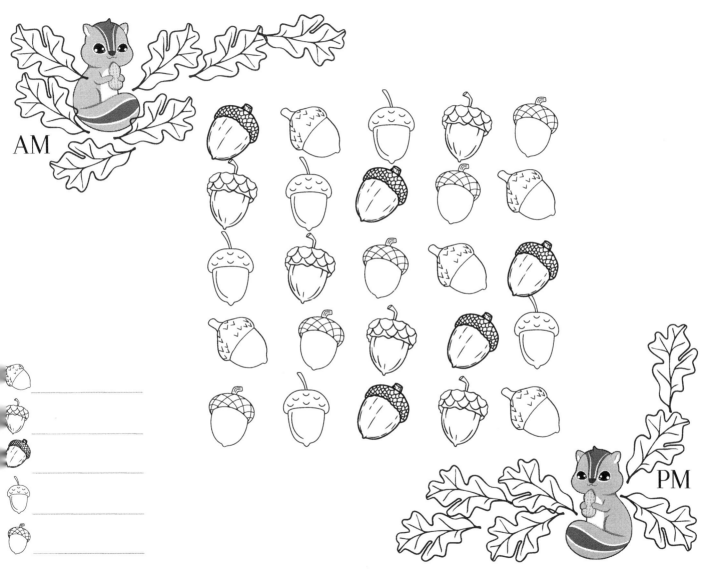

Date

What

How

How Many Times

What

How

How Many Times

What

How

How Many Times

Listen Like a Maniac!

Questions for next Lesson?

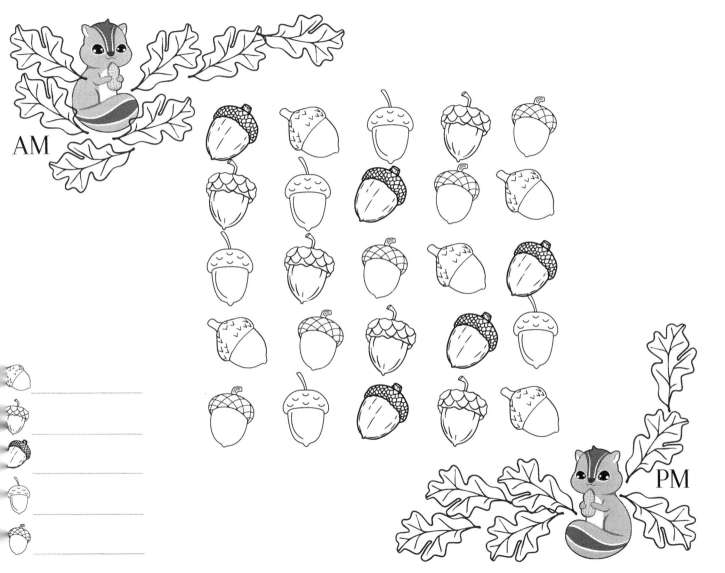

AM

PM

Date

What

How

How Many Times

What

How

How Many Times

What

How

How Many Times

Listen Like a Maniac!

Questions for next Lesson?

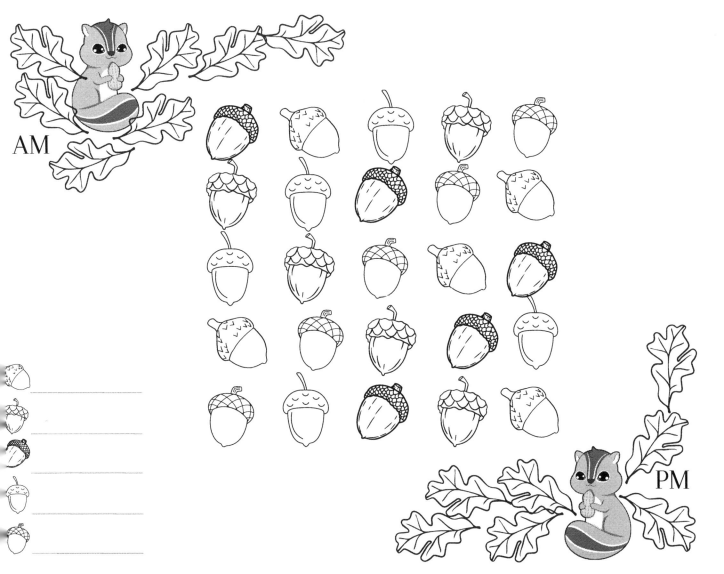

Date

What

How

How Many Times

What

How

How Many Times

What

How

How Many Times

Questions for next Lesson?

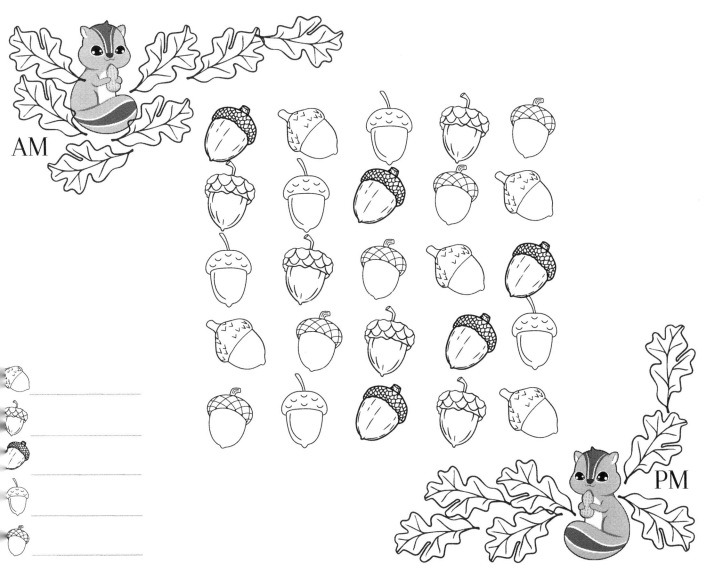

Date

What

How

How Many Times

What

How

How Many Times

What

How

How Many Times

Listen Like a Maniac!

Questions for next Lesson?

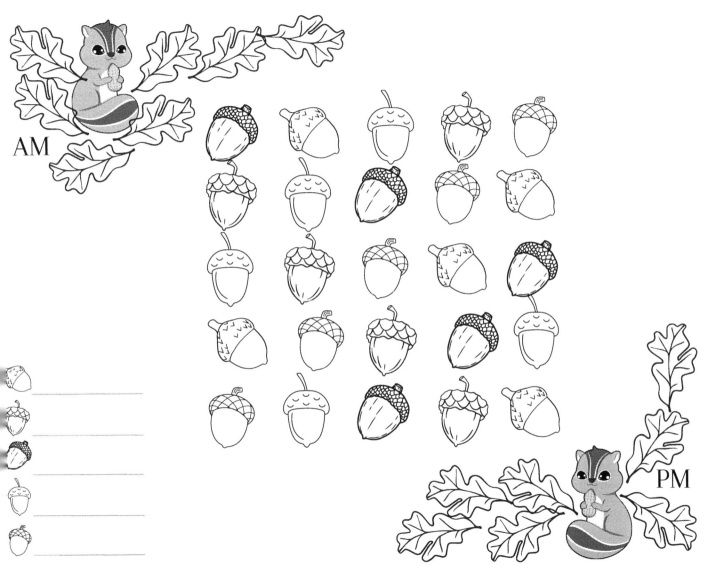

Date

What

How

How Many Times

What

How

How Many Times

What

How

How Many Times

Listen Like a Maniac!

Questions for next Lesson?

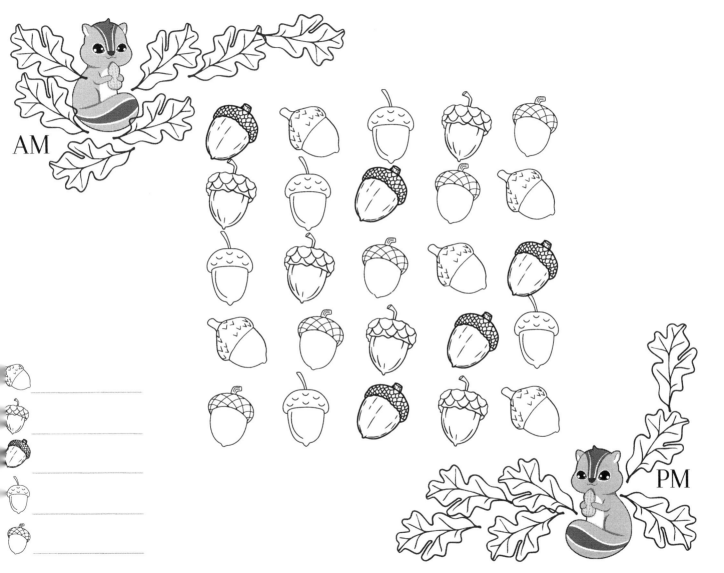

Date

What

How

How Many Times

What

How

How Many Times

What

How

How Many Times

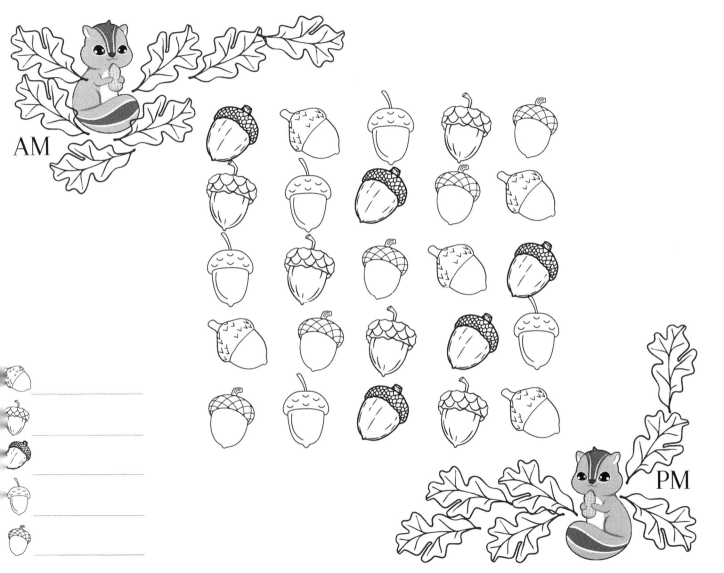

AM

PM

Date

What

How

How Many Times

What

How

How Many Times

What

How

How Many Times

♪♪ Listen Like a Maniac!

Questions for next Lesson?

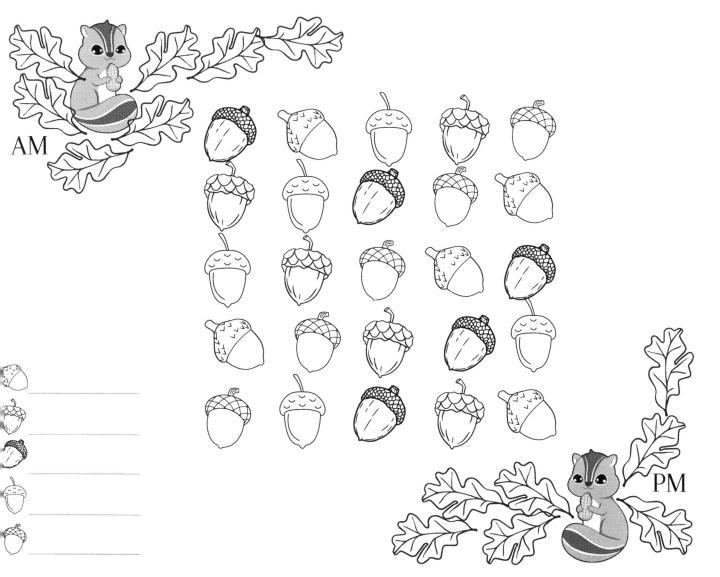

Date _____

What

How

How Many Times

What

How

How Many Times

What

How

How Many Times

Listen Like a Maniac!

Questions for next Lesson?

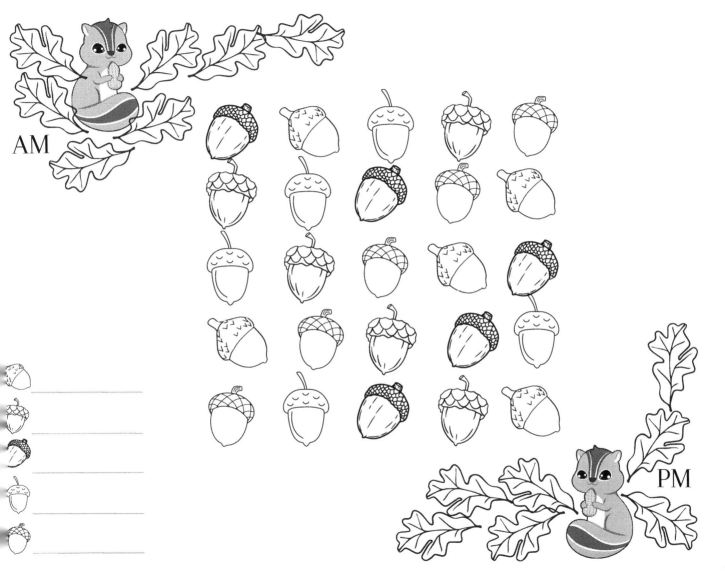

AM

PM

Date

What

How

How Many Times

What

How

How Many Times

What

How

How Many Times

Questions for next Lesson?

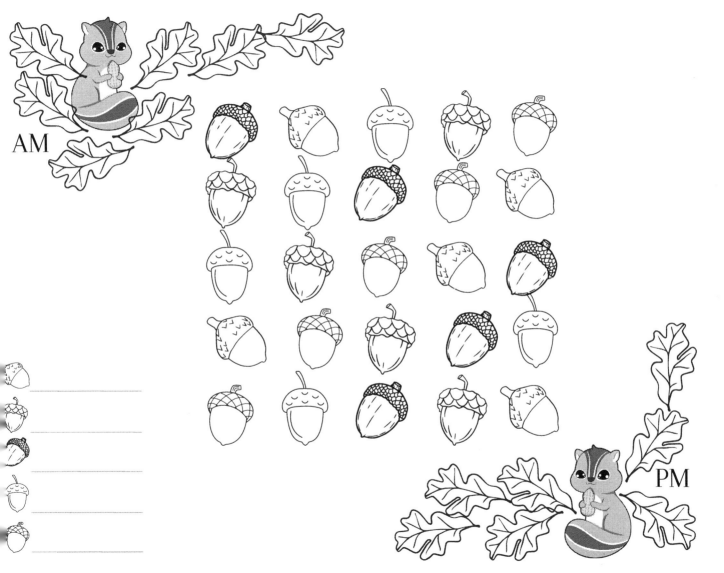

Date

What

How

How Many Times

What

How

How Many Times

What

How

How Many Times

♪♫ Listen Like a Maniac!

Questions for next Lesson?

My Wish List

WRITE YOUR GOALS HERE
THEY CAN BE PIECES THAT YOU WANT TO PLAY OR SKILLS TO PERFECT,
CHECK BACK HERE EVERY ONCE IN A WHILE
TO SEE HOW CLOSE YOU ARE GETTING!

My Aha Moments

Ready for Recital

LIST YOUR POLISHED PIECES HERE -
IF SOMEONE SAYS "PLAY SOMETHING" AND YOUR MIND GOES BLANK,
YOU CAN JUST FLIP OPEN THIS PAGE AND HAVE A LOOK!

Made in the USA
Columbia, SC
26 June 2023

19164577R00061